QUESTIONS AND ANSWERS ON MATHEMATICS

For first year university and high school students

Volume One

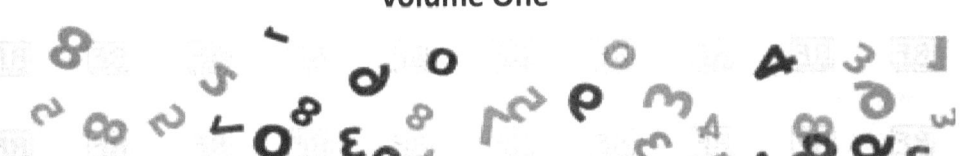

INTRODUCTION

This is the first edition of questions and answers on mathematics. It is designed to help students with understanding of mathematics.

First year students in universities and high school students will find it handy during revisions.

Questions and answers on mathematics will show you step by step how to solve mathematical questions.

Some of the topics covered in this edition include surds, quadratic equations, indices, logarithms, vectors, functions and relations.

For questions and comments, leave a message on

basic2tech@gmail.com

QUESTION 1a

The function $f : x \rightarrow \dfrac{3x - 5}{x + 1}$

i.   Determine $f^{-1}(x)$

ii.   Calculate the value of x, if $f(x) = 15$

iii.   Determine the value for x, for which:

     i. $f(x) = 0$

     ii. $f(x)$ is undefined.

SOLUTION TO QUESTION 1a

i. $f: x \rightarrow \dfrac{3x - 5}{x + 1}$

$f: x$ Becomes $f(x)$

$f(x) = \dfrac{3x - 5}{x + 1}$

$f(x) = y$; so we substitute $f(x)$ for y

Therefore; $y = \dfrac{3x - 5}{x + 1}$

SOLUTION TO QUESTION 1a

Interchange y for x, and x for y

$x = \dfrac{3y - 5}{y + 1}$;   Cross multiplication gives;

$x(y + 1) = 3y - 5$

$xy + x = 3y - 5$

Collecting like terms;

$x + 5 = 3y - xy$

SOLUTION TO QUESTION 1a

Factorizing the right hand side, the equation becomes;

$$x + 5 = y(3 - x)$$

We make y the subject of formulae. It becomes;

$$y = \frac{x + 5}{3 - x}$$

Therefore the answer is;

$$f^{-1}(x) = \frac{x + 5}{3 - x}$$

QUESTION 1a

ii. $\quad f(x) = 15$

$\qquad$ Remember $f(x) = \dfrac{3x - 5}{x + 1}$

$\dfrac{3x - 5}{x + 1} = 15$

Cross multiplication;

$3x - 5 = 15x + 15$

Collect like terms;

$3x - 15x = 15 + 5$

SOLUTION TO QUESTION 1a

$$-12x = 20$$

Dividing both sides by -12

$$x = -\frac{20}{12}$$

$$x = -{}^5/_3$$

SOLUTION TO QUESTION 1a

iii. $f(x) = 0$

$$\frac{3x - 5}{x + 1} = 0$$

Cross Multiplication gives;

$3x - 5 = 0$

$3x = 5$

Dividing both sides by $3x$, we get;

$x = {}^5/_3$

SOLUTION TO QUESTION 1a

iv. $f^{-1}(x)$ is undefined.

Note: For $f^{-1}(x)$ to be undefined, we have to equate the denominator of $f^{-1}(x) = 0$

Remember, $f^{-1}(x) = \dfrac{x + 5}{3 - x}$

Therefore, $3 - x = 0$

$3 = x$

$x = 3$

QUESTION 1b

i. $6x^2 + 9x - 6 = 0$

Using factorizing method;

First multiply the coefficient of x^2 with the constant;

$6 x - 6 = -36$

Think of two factors of 36,

Whose product equals -36 and whose sum equals $+9x$

The two factors are $-3x \; and + 12x$

SOLUTION TO QUESTION 1b

Replace $+9x$ with $-3x + 12x$; the equation becomes;

$6x^2 - 3x + 12x - 6 = 0$

$(6x^2 - 3x)(12x - 6) = 0$;   Factorizing the equation, we get;

$3x(2x - 1) + 6(2x - 1) = 0$;

$(3x + 6)(2x - 1) = 0$;   Equating each equation to zero gives;

$3x + 6 = 0$

SOLUTION TO QUESTION 1b

$3x = -6$

Dividing both sides by $3x$ gives;

$x = {}^{-6}/_3 = -2$

Also;

$2x - 1 = 0$

$2x = 1$

Dividing both sides by 2x gives;

$x = {}^1/_2$

So $x = -2$ or ${}^1/_2$

SOLUTION TO QUESTION 1b

ii. $x^2 - 2x - 8 = 0$

Using Factorization method

Please follow the steps as stated above;

$x^2 + 2x - 4x - 8 = 0$

$(x^2 + 2x) - (4x + 8) = 0$

$x(x + 2) - 4(x + 2) = 0$

$(x - 4)(x + 2) = 0$

Quadratic Equations

SOLUTION TO QUESTION 1b

$x - 4 = 0$

$x = 4$

Also;

$x + 2 = 0|$

$x = -2$

Therefore $x = 4 \; or -2$

QUESTION 2a

Express the following without logs: $\log x = \log p + 4\log q - 2$

SOLUTION

Note that; $2 = 2\log 10$

This is true because $2\log 10 = 1$ so the original equation becomes;

$\log x = \log p + 4\log q - 2\log 10$

Remember: $y\log x = \log x^y$ therefore the above equation becomes;

$\log x = \log p + \log q^4 - \log 10^2$

SOLUTION TO QUESTION 2a Cont

$$\log x = \log p + \log q^4 - \log 100$$

Applying the laws of log; $\log a + \log b = \log ab$

$$\log a - \log b = \log \frac{a}{b}$$

Therefore our equation becomes;

$$\log x = \log \left(\frac{pq^4}{100}\right)$$

SOLUTION TO QUESTION 2a Cont

Cancelling the log from both sides, we are left with;

$$x = \frac{pq^4}{100}$$

QUESTION 2b

Express in log form: $f = \dfrac{1}{d\sqrt{LC}}$

SOLUTION

First we take the log of both sides;

$$\log f = \log\left(\frac{1}{d(LC)^{1/2}}\right)$$

Applying the law of log as shown in question 2a;

SOLUTION TO QUESTION 2b cont

$$\log f = \log 1 - \log d + \log(LC)^{1/2}$$

Therefore in log form;

$$\log f = \log 1 - \log d + \frac{1}{2}\log LC$$

QUESTION 2c

$$if \begin{cases} A = 5i + 4j + 2k \\ B = 4i - 5j + 3k \\ C = 2i - j - 2k \end{cases}$$

Determine the value of $A.B$ and the angle between the vectors A and B

SOLUTION

Remember $A.B = A_i \times B_i + A_j \times B_j + A_k \times B_k$

So; $A.B = (5 \times 4) + (4 \times -5) + (2 \times 3)$

$A.B = 20 - 20 + 6$

$A.B = 6$

SOLUTION TO QUESTION 2c cont

To get the angle between the vectors,

$$\cos \theta = \frac{A.B}{|A||B|}$$

$$\theta = \cos^{-1} \frac{A.B}{|A||B|}$$

To get $|A|$; we find the resultant of vector A;

$$|A| = \sqrt{5^2 + 4^2 + 2^2}$$

$$|A| = \sqrt{25 + 16 + 4} = \sqrt{45}$$

$$|A| = 6.7082$$

SOLUTION TO QUESTION 2c cont

In the same way, we get $|B|$

$$|B| = \sqrt{4^2 + (-5)^2 + 3^2}$$

$$|B| = \sqrt{16 + 25 + 9} = \sqrt{50}$$

$$|B| = 7.0711$$

Vectors

SOLUTION TO QUESTION 2c cont

Therefore, the angle between the vectors is;

$$\theta = \cos^{-1} \frac{6}{6.7082 \times 7.0711}$$

$$\theta = \cos^{-1} \frac{6}{47.4344}$$

$$\theta = \cos^{-1} 0.1265$$

$$\theta = 82.7°$$

QUESTION 2d

Simplify $\sqrt{\left(a^{\frac{7}{3}}b^5c^{\frac{-2}{3}}\right)} \div \sqrt[3]{\left(a^{\frac{1}{2}}b^3c^{-1}\right)}$

SOLUTION

Remember laws of indices; $\sqrt{x} = (x)^{\frac{1}{2}}$; and $\sqrt[3]{x} = (x)^{\frac{1}{3}}$

So applying the laws above, we get;

$\left(a^{\frac{7}{3}}b^5c^{\frac{-2}{3}}\right)^{\frac{1}{2}} \div \left(a^{\frac{1}{2}}b^3c^{-1}\right)^{\frac{1}{3}}$

Indices

SOLUTION TO QUESTION 2d cont

Next step is to multiply the power outside the bracket;

By all the powers inside the bracket;

$$a^{\frac{7}{3}} b^{\frac{5}{2}} c^{\frac{-1}{3}} \div a^{\frac{1}{6}} b^{\frac{1}{9}} c^{\frac{-1}{3}}$$

Also another law of indices; $a^x \div a^y = a^{x-y}$

We apply this law, we get;

$$a^{\frac{7}{3} - \frac{1}{6}} \; b^{\frac{5}{2} - \frac{1}{9}} \; c^{\frac{-1}{3} + \frac{1}{3}}$$ Please note the change of sign for c.

SOLUTION TO QUESTION 2d cont

Simplifying further, we get;

$a^1 b^{\frac{3}{2}} c^0$ From the law of indices, $c^0 = 1$

$ab^{\frac{3}{2}}$ or $a\sqrt{b^3}$

QUESTION 3a

Rationalize the following and simplify

i. $\dfrac{1}{\sqrt{3}-1}$

ii. $\dfrac{1}{2\sqrt{5}+3}$

iii. $\dfrac{1}{2\sqrt{3}+\sqrt{2}}$

iv. $\dfrac{1}{\sqrt{6}-\sqrt{5}}$

v. $\dfrac{1}{\sqrt{2}+1} + \dfrac{1}{\sqrt{2}-1}$

SOLUTION TO QUESTION 3a

i. $\dfrac{1}{\sqrt{3}-1}$

To rationalize, we multiply the numerator and denominator;

By the conjugate of the denominator;

Conjugate is done by changing the sign between two terms;

The conjugate of $\sqrt{3} - 1$ is $\sqrt{3} + 1$, so;

$$\dfrac{1}{\sqrt{3}-1} \times \dfrac{\sqrt{3}+1}{\sqrt{3}+1}$$

Surds

SOLUTION TO QUESTION 3a cont

$$\frac{\sqrt{3}+1}{(\sqrt{3}-1)(\sqrt{3}+1)};$$

Remember; $\left(\sqrt{a}+b\right)\left(\sqrt{a}-b\right) = \left(\sqrt{a}\right)^2 - (b)^2;$

Therefore the equation becomes;

$$\frac{\sqrt{3}+1}{\left(\sqrt{3}\right)^2 - 1^2} = \frac{\sqrt{3}+1}{3-1}$$

$$\frac{\sqrt{3}+1}{2} = \frac{\sqrt{3}}{2} + \frac{1}{2}$$

SOLUTION TO QUESTION 3a cont

i. $\dfrac{1}{2\sqrt{5}+3}$

Using the same steps as outline in 3i;

The conjugate of $2\sqrt{5} + 3$ is $2\sqrt{5} - 3$

$$\dfrac{1}{2\sqrt{5}+3} \times \dfrac{2\sqrt{5}-3}{2\sqrt{5}-3}$$

$$\dfrac{2\sqrt{5}-3}{(2\sqrt{5}+3)(2\sqrt{5}-3)} = \dfrac{2\sqrt{5}-3}{(2\sqrt{5})^2-3^2};$$

$$\dfrac{2\sqrt{5}-3}{20-9} = \dfrac{2\sqrt{5}-3}{11}$$

$$\dfrac{2\sqrt{5}}{11} - \dfrac{3}{11}$$

Surds

SOLUTION TO QUESTION 3a cont

iii. $\dfrac{1}{2\sqrt{3}+\sqrt{2}}$

The conjugate of $2\sqrt{3}+\sqrt{2}$ is $2\sqrt{3}-\sqrt{2}$

So rationalizing;

$$\dfrac{1}{2\sqrt{3}+\sqrt{2}} \times \dfrac{2\sqrt{3}-\sqrt{2}}{2\sqrt{3}-\sqrt{2}};$$

$$\dfrac{2\sqrt{3}-\sqrt{2}}{(2\sqrt{3}+\sqrt{2})(2\sqrt{3}-\sqrt{2})} = \dfrac{2\sqrt{3}-\sqrt{2}}{(2\sqrt{3})^2-(\sqrt{2})^2};$$

$$\dfrac{2\sqrt{3}-\sqrt{2}}{12-2} = \dfrac{2\sqrt{3}-\sqrt{2}}{10};$$

$$\dfrac{2\sqrt{3}}{10} - \dfrac{\sqrt{2}}{10} = \dfrac{\sqrt{3}}{5} - \dfrac{\sqrt{2}}{10}.$$

Surds

SOLUTION TO QUESTION 3a cont

iv.　　$\dfrac{1}{\sqrt{6}-\sqrt{5}}$

The conjugate of $\sqrt{6} - \sqrt{5}$ is $\sqrt{6} + \sqrt{5}$

So rationalizing;

$$\dfrac{1}{\sqrt{6}-\sqrt{5}} \times \dfrac{\sqrt{6}+\sqrt{5}}{\sqrt{6}+\sqrt{5}};$$

$$\dfrac{\sqrt{6}+\sqrt{5}}{(\sqrt{6}-\sqrt{5})(\sqrt{6}+\sqrt{5})} = \dfrac{\sqrt{6}+\sqrt{5}}{(\sqrt{6})^2-(\sqrt{5})^2};$$

$$\dfrac{\sqrt{6}+\sqrt{5}}{6-5} = \sqrt{6} + \sqrt{5}.$$

SOLUTION TO QUESTION 3a cont

v. $\dfrac{1}{\sqrt{2}+1} + \dfrac{1}{\sqrt{2}-1}$

Finding the L.C.M it becomes;

$$\dfrac{\sqrt{2}-1+\sqrt{2}+1}{(\sqrt{2}+1)(\sqrt{2}-1)} = \dfrac{2\sqrt{2}}{(\sqrt{2})^2-(1)^2};$$

$$\dfrac{2\sqrt{2}}{2-1} = 2\sqrt{2};$$

Surds

QUESTION 3b

Solve the equation: $2(2^{2x}) - 5(2^x) + 2 = 0$

SOLUTION

The equation can be rewritten as;

$$2(2^x)^2 - 5(2^x) + 2 = 0$$

Let $2^x = y$ so the equation becomes;

$2y^2 - 5y + 2 = 0$; This is a quadratic equation.

SOLUTION TO QUESTION 3b cont

Please review the steps in question 1b.

$$2y^2 - 4y - y + 2 = 0;$$

$$(2y^2 - 4y)(-y + 2) = 0$$

Factorizing we get;

$$2y(y - 2) - 1(y - 2) = 0$$

$$(2y - 1)(y - 2) = 0$$

SOLUTION TO QUESTION 3b cont

Equating both equations to zero;

$$2y - 1 = 0; \quad y - 2 = 0$$

$$2y = 1; \quad\quad\quad y = 2$$

$$y = \frac{1}{2}$$

Indicial Equation

SOLUTION TO QUESTION 3b cont

So to get x, we substitute the values of y into $2^x = y$

$$2^x = \frac{1}{2}; \qquad also \qquad 2^x = 2$$

$$2^x = 2^{-1} \qquad and \qquad 2^x = 2^1$$

Cancelling the base on both sides;

$$x = -1 \qquad and \qquad x = 1$$

Indicial Equation

QUESTION 3c

Solve the simultaneous equation: $\begin{cases} \log_x y = 2 \\ xy = 8 \end{cases}$

SOLUTION

$\log_x y = 2$ ... $equation\ 1$

$xy = 8$ .... $equation\ 2$

From equation 1;

$\log_x y = 2$

Simultaneous Equation

SOLUTION TO QUESTION 3c cont

Changing the log to indices equation;

$$y = x^2 \text{ ... } equation\ 3$$

Insert equation $y = x^2$ into equation 2. It gives;

$$x(x^2) = 8$$

$$x^3 = 8$$

SOLUTION TO QUESTION 3c cont

Taking the cube root of both sides;

$$\sqrt[3]{x^3} = \sqrt[3]{8};$$

Note: On the left hand side, the cube cancels out the cube root;

So we are left with;

$$x = \sqrt[3]{8}$$

$$x = 2$$

SOLUTION TO QUESTION 3c cont

To get y, we insert $x = 2$ into equation 3

So, $y = x^2$; become;

$y = 2^2$

$y = 4$

Therefore; $x = 2$, $y = 4$

SOLUTION TO QUESTION 3c cont

NOTE: you can double check by inserting the;

Values of x and y into the equations;

Let's check by doing so for equation 1,

$\log_x y = 2$

$x = 2, y = 4.$

So; $\log_2 4 = \log_2 2^2$

$2\log_2 2$

Simultaneous Equation

SOLUTION TO QUESTION 3c cont

Remember form log, $\log_2 2 = 1$

So $2\log_2 2 = 2 \times 1 = 2$

This shows that we are correct.

MESSAGE FROM THE AUTHOR

I hope you enjoyed this first volume. Watch out for volume 2. For questions and comments leave a message on basic2tech@gmail.com.

Also if there are topics you want to be covered in our next edition or questions you want solved, you are free to drop it on the email above.

www.ingramcontent.com/pod-product-compliance
Lightning Source LLC
Chambersburg PA
CBHW051404280526

45784CB00007B/3094